We Need to Get It Right or It Will Be Tight

MARY RUMBLE FLEMMING

We Need to Get It Right or It Will Be Tight
Copyright © 2024 by Mary Rumble Flemming

ISBN: 978-1639458448 (hc)
ISBN: 978-1639458349 (sc)
ISBN: 978-163945-8356 (e)

All rights reserved. No part of this publication may be reproduced, distributed, or transmitted in any form or by any means, including photocopying, recording, or other electronic or mechanical methods, without the prior written permission of the publisher and/or the author, except in the case of brief quotations embodied in critical reviews and other noncommercial uses permitted by copyright law.

The views expressed in this book are solely those of the author and do not necessarily reflect the views of the publisher, and the publisher hereby disclaims any responsibility for them.

Writers' Branding
(877) 608-6550
www.writersbranding.com
media@writersbranding.com

Table of Contents

Do You Want the Earth To Sing? 1
Is Your Egg Cracked 2
Comparing 3
Sun Shine 4
Shake A Hand 5
One Way 6
Toss A Coin 7
Dirt, or Topsoil 8
Challenge 9
Narrow minded people 10
Around A Tree 11
Tic or Tac 12
Frontline 13
Humpty Dumpty 14
Children Today 15
God Will Carry Me 16
We Need to Get It Right, ... 17
Or It Will Be Tight 17
Who Is In Your Box? 19
Why Not Be Humble 21
Just Like A Crab 22
HOPSCOTCH 23
What's Your Joke? 24
What Is Your Mountain In Your Life? 25
FOOT SOLDIER 26
Don't Make A U-Turn 27
How To Love God's Child 28
The Earth Will Tell 29
Who Do You Report To? 30
Ditches 31
RAW 32
Don't Let Your Back-bend 33

I hope that this book will help people to understand the time in which we are living. Not everyone goes to church or a place to worship. Just to think, if you are not happy with things in the World, How do you think God feels (God can change this creation, but we have to want God to change the world). We as people need to change our hearts. Everyone wants to go to heaven; do you really think you will go to heaven by treating other people the way you do? This book is not sugar-coded, ***"Raw. Do you want the earth to sing, We need to get right or it will be tight."*** I want people to really focus on how life will be if we do not turn to God and repent. We as a nation need to put our focus back on God and not on what the world wants or has to say about life. What does God's word say about life and how we should do things? Some people may find some critical aspects about this book. So, what are you doing in your life to help make this world a better place to live by God's word?

Do You Want the Earth To Sing?

If we as people do not praise God
The earth will take our place and sing
People will not know what season we are in

Warning comes before a destruction
And every man has a choice to repent
If man do not repent
The earth will take your place and sing

The flood came, it rained for forty days and forty nights
Only the ones in the ark survive
No one know God's plan, it could be joy or pain
Lot's wife turned into a pillar of salt when she looked back
Only God knows what is in every man's heart

Man can destroy each other
But man cannot destroy the earth
If man repent and turn from their evil ways

The earth will sing a joyful whisper of grace
If man do not repent The earth will rain fire and brimstone

Is Your Egg Cracked

An egg can be like a person or what goes on in one's life
A person has seven layers of skin before you get to the bone.
An egg has eight different coats before you get to the yoke.

> What happens when that egg falls, if it is a hard fall it will break into many pieces?
> What's inside the egg, will come out it can be solid, or it can ooze out

When a person is having a hard time, and they don't have God in their life, they can feel as if they're cracking up or falling apart
This is how things flow when we don't have God in our life
With God in your life, it will flow much easier

> A boil egg, when it falls it will crack, but not into many pieces
> When you peel the shell off that egg, it still holds firm

That boil egg is like a person that totally has God in their life.
When hard times come, it is their prayers, faith and trust in God, that helps them to stand strong
The security of knowing that God is in control of everything

Comparing

Will you compare an orange to an apple, or a dog to a cow?
Why do people like to compare one person to another?

An orange peeling is thick,
Just as a person can have a challenging personality
An apple peeling is thin,
Just as a person can have a quiet, or meek personality

Comparing a person to another can bring pain, it can cause jealousy, competition or envy
It can also cause shyness, low self- esteem, fear, sad to say even depression.
I thank God for what His words say

> 1 Corinthians 4:7 (NKJV)
>
> *For who makes you differ from another? And what do you have that you did not receive? Now if you did indeed receive it, why do you boast as if you had not received it?*

Sun Shine

God bless us to enjoy the sun shine, oh it can feel, so great
You can feel the warmth, and see the beauty
How the sun shine on me, it may not shine on you the same

God bless us with the Holy spirit,
How the Holy Spirit touch me, will not touch you the same

The sun is a blessing from God, it helps us to know the different in day and night
The sun allows everything to grow, with some plants the more sun light the more it grows

The more you read God words, the Holy Bible the more you should know God's word is here for everyone,
God bless us with life, it is up to you to seek God's plan for your life.

Shake A Hand

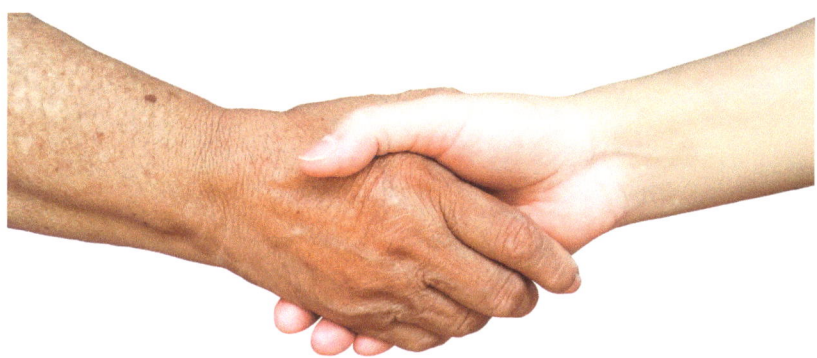

Matthew {18:19}

Again, I say unto you, That if two of you shall agree on earth as touching anything that they shall ask, it shall be done for them of my Father which is in heaven.

It is not just man's world.
It is God's World for all men to enjoy

2 Chronicles {7:14}

*If my people, which are called by my name,
shall humble themselves, and pray, and seek
my face, and turn from their wicked way; then
I will hear from heaven, and will forgive
their sin, and will heal their land.*

There is over 2,000 different Religion in the World, sad to say two hundred or more can not Touch and agree that things in the world need to be better.

Shake a hand touch and agree, fighting is not getting the world anywhere.

One Way

One man might think that he holds all the cards
Because he is rich and that gives him the right to control everything
Being very bold

> One way
> One life to live
> One master plan, God

This is God's World, people are here to enjoy this world, not to kill each other One way, God way

> Philippians {2:10 and 11}
>
> *[10] That at the name of Jesus every knee should bow, of things in heaven, and things in earth, and things under the earth*
> *[11] And "that every tongue should confess that Jesus Christ is Lord, to the glory of God the Father."*

Toss A Coin

Toss a coin flip a coin roll the coin around
Shine a coin spin a coin don't let it touch the ground
Just like a person always running not sure what they want
They will run here turn around and run again not really sure what they are looking for

Shine a coin spin a coin don't let it touch the ground
Toss a coin flip a coin roll the coin around
That coin might go from one hand to another, that coin will always be solid and be a coin It can not increase it value

It is a good thing to let our mind expand, even to be optimistic
And to keep your personality the same, not to display an egotistical personality
Remember that coin still remains the same regardless of who's pocket it touch

So, if you have a penny personality why do you think you are so much better if you touch that quarter of fifty cent, no one is better than the other
We are all the same in the sight of God, He still loves us the same
All your coins spend and add value to the other

Dirt, or Topsoil

A lot of things grow from dirt and topsoil, all vegetable, trees, grass, and flowers
All animals eats what is on the ground, or what is grown in the earth
The ground is dirt, topsoil is dirt

Mammals, some of them eat from the ground,
So we all love dirt, because we got to eat

Soil comes in five different shades, black, brown, red, gray and white
You can mix the soil and get other colors
Clay is the smallest soil particle

> Genesis {2:7}
>
> *And the Lord God formed man of the dust of the ground, and breathed into his nostrils the breath of life; and man became a living soul.*

So many people might say they heard that before,
well we need to hear it again everyone was form from dirt.
So why does one dirt think that it is better than the other dirt,
why do one dirt dislike the color of another dirt?

Challenge

Why do some people like to challenge others?
Sometimes it might because they are trying to learn something
Sports event is when most people love to see the difference which is fine

The person that loves to challenge everyone, need to challenge themselves
They don't realize they are walking on shaky ground and they need to move around
For surely one day someone will come and challenge them the same way

No one is the best at everything they do, nor right about the things they say
If they were accurate about everything, then why are you here on earth
We all are a work in progress, no man on earth is a 100%

If you keep challenging a person, people can look at you as being offense and insecure
If you are a person that love to challenge others and you do not work in the same arena
Would you love for someone to keep questioning you, about the task you need to accomplish? Do you compliment others on things they have accomplished?

Hebrews {3:13}

But exhort one another daily, while it is called To day; lest any of you be hardened through the deceitfulness of sin

Narrow minded people

People with narrow minds is afraid of the unknown
Fear is not knowing of understanding

People have been on earth since the beginning of time
So have prejudice, you will think that people would had gotten accustomed to one another
No matter the color

If it is not part of the solution than it is a problem
We all need God in our life to help us to solve this issue

People let the devil control them, thinking racism is ok
If you think racism is fine, you will not make it into heaven by thinking this way

> Genesis {1: 27}
>
> *So God created man in his own image, in the image of God he created him; male and female he created them.*
>
> I John {4:20-21}
>
> *[20] If a man says, I love God, and hateth his brother, he is a liar: for he that loveth not his brother whom he hath seen, how can he love God whom he hath not seen?*
> *[21] And this commandment have we from him, that he who loveth God love his brother also.*

Around A Tree

Around a tree and back again
A baby will cry over spilt milk because
the baby doesn't know that it can be replace
With love and nutrition, the child will grow

If you go around the tree again, not realizing how much strength it has taken out of you
In life a person keeps trying the same thing over and over again getting the same results

Not realizing they might need to change the way they do things
If it is not working, you might want to do something different

After time we might pray to God and asked God to help us
We ask God to take control but we want it our way
We got to have faith and know that God is in charge

Tic or Tac

Tic or tac

   I make you mad, so you try to pay me back

     That is a childish game, it is truly ashamed

       Everyone has feeling, and no one enjoys being hurt

      Sad to say in life there will be pain

       The devil knows his time will soon be up

        So, people now are doing some crazy things

We need to stop tic or tac

  Get on our knees and pray to God

    For blessing comes from God, who is in heaven above

      Blessing from God is something the whole world need plenty of

Frontline

Frontline is the people that stay prayerful for everything,
    Things that are going on in the world
        The Church should be the frontline, sad to say some churches are blind
        Because they are following what the world says,
Use the Holy Bible to show you the truth, of what God's word say about life
Stand strong in God's word, it can change this sinful world

    2 Chronicles {7:14}

If my people, which are called by my name, shall humble themselves, and pray, and seek my face, and turn from their wicked ways; then will I hear from heaven, and will forgive their sin, and will heal their land.

Sad some people might say they do not pray, nor do they believe in God
        People that have evil ways, still want prayer
They may not want deliverance, nor repentance from their sin
We can not change the way our heart beat, nor the color of our blood
    But we can change what is in our heart

We Need to Get It Right or It Will Be Tight

Humpty Dumpty

Humpty Dumpty sat on the wall, Humpty Dumpty had a great fall
The world can be like Humpty Dumpty, it will have a great fall.
If the people in the world do not change their ways
People living in their sinful ways, not realizing there is a price to pay.
That price is your very own soul, no one is promise to live to see another day

Some people are tired of what's happening in the world today
Not really understanding that God can be tired of the sin that is going on today.

Yes, God can do something about the world, however man need to repent.
We need to look to God for all things
Are you living by man plans, or by what God's words says?

> Jeremiah {18:7 and 8}
>
> *[7] At what instant I shall speak concerning a nation, and concerning a kingdom, to pluck up, and pull down, and to destroy it;*
>
> *[8] "If that nation, against whom I have pronounced, turn from their evil, I will repent of the evil that I thought to do unto them.*

Children Today

Parents today need to teach their child to pray, it will be an admired thing.
Some parents do a wonderful job with their children
Parents that are in charge, their child will be respectful to others

The children are our future, if we train them well today it will help this world to become a better place
Parents who live a Godly life, may God bless their children to live a successful life

A child that a parent cannot say no to leaves you thinking who is the one in control
Every child needs a strong foundation, stability and to know they are loved
We need to take a stand, guide the children in the right direction
This is God's plans

> Proverb {23:13}
>
> *Withhold not correction from the child: for if thou beatest him with the rod, he shall not die*
>
> Proverb {13:24}
>
> *He that spareth his rod hated his son: but he that loveth him chasteneth him betimes.*

God Will Carry Me

OH my God I have walk through the rain, and through the snow
for I know you are with me
For my secret enemies try to keep me by their side (for the enemies
that you don't know)
God, I know that I have to keep my faith in you
For with God all things are possible I got to stay strong keep my
faith and pray to God
OH my God for I know that you will bless me to keep the devil
under my feet for the devil try
to rise, he did not realize that I am God's child and that God's
angels surround me
I felt the rushing strength of the wind, the streaming dry heat of the
desert
That is the pain we may face in life
It is how we endure life challenges, this will help to build our faith,
and know
God is there for you

We Need to Get It Right,

Or It Will Be Tight

We need to get it right, or it will be tight.
People need to turn to God and ask for repentance,
with all that is going on in the World today
If you do not know to pray, you might not truly be safe

In the sport arena everybody knows how to play by rules,
on this earth life is not a game, God has rules
We can live by God rules by letting the Holy Bible guide you,
or you can die by them by not living by the Holy Bible

> John {8:44}
>
> *"Ye are of your father the devil, and the lust of your father ye will do. He was a murderer from the beginning, and abode not in the truth, because there is no truth in him. When he speaketh a lie, he speaketh of his own: for he is a liar, and the father or it."*
>
> Jeremiah {10:10}
>
> *But the Lord is the true God, He is the living God, and an everlasting king: at his wrath the earth shall tremble, and the nations shall not be able to abide his indignation.*

If you want to keep playing man ways, telling lies, killing, stealing, adultery etc., and bringing destruction, in this world we fail to realize we will be judged by God's Holy words.

> Revelation {2:21}
>
> *And I gave her space to repent of her fornication; and she repented not.*

Revelation {2:22}

Behold, I will cast her into a bed, and them that commit adultery with her into great tribulation, except they repent of their deeds.

Revelation {2:23}

And I will kill her children with death; and all the churches shall know that I am he which searcheth the reins and hearts: and I will give unto every one you according to your works.

Who Is In Your Box?

Jack is not the only one in the box
How full is your box!!
Box of religion
Box of tradition

Touch the knob with your hand
It still does not solve the problem of abuse
Box of confusion

Wind it up or down, wind it around and you will find
A Box of selfishness
A Box of pride

Just as Jack is close in a box so can some people be close in a box
They cannot think outside the box

When the song is finish playing
Jack pops out, he is so surprise, of what he sees
People can be the same way
Stop trying to control others

Putting limitations on what the word of GOD says

Let the Holy Spirit flow
Who's in your box
What is in your box
Let the Holy Spirit Flow

Hosea {4:6}

My people are destroyed for the lack of knowledge; because thou hast rejected knowledge, I will also reject thee, that thou shalt be no priest to me: seeing thou hast forgotten the law of thy GOD, I will also forget thy children.

Mark {7:13}

Making the word of God of none effect through your tradition, which ye have delivered: and many such like things do ye

Why Not Be Humble

> *(James {4:10} Humble yourself in the sight of the Lord, and He should lift you up)*

In life we should be or need to be humble to people.
People on our jobs, family or friends, even a stranger,
This can be God's plan.

When selfishness over takes you and everything in your life began to crumble
Then you will realize that you need to be humble.

By humbling yourself that do not mean that you have fumble in life
This will not render you the world's favor
Humbling yourself for a Godly cause will give you God's favor

> *(1 Peter {5:6} Humble yourselves therefore under the mighty hand of God, that He may exalt you in due time)*

Just Like A Crab

        Like crabs in a bucket, when one crab makes it to the top
        Two or three crabs will pull it down
        Just as a person will try to pull another person down
        If you know who is trying to pull you down Just move around
        The more you move the less the others will know
        There is no doubt, out of fear a crab will always pull another crab down
        Out of fear a person will do the same thing.
    If you feel that you are being pull down Remember to move around, And what God words say

(Matthew {6:3} But when thou doest alms, let not thy left hand know what thy right hand doeth:)

HOPSCOTCH

Hopscotch
     One
        Two
           Three
It's not just a child game
In life you need to treat people the way you want to be treated
Hopping to one, two and three
Knowing at four and five both feet have to be planted on solid ground

Like in life when you go through hard times
Sometimes you might say to yourself, if I can get both feet planted on solid ground
You need to be careful how you treat people, because what you say can so easier turn around to you

Hopping again hoping to get to the end
Turn around and you will see the same numbers again

Because in life you can see the same thing happening to you
When you talk about someone

Galatians {6:7} Be not deceived; God is not mocked: for soever a man soweth, that shall he also reap

What's Your Joke?

An inside joke can be outside pain
    A private joke can be outside shame
        We all can be guilty of one or the other
            Thank God because He knows everyone's heart
                He takes the bitter with the sweet and let everyone have their part

Even a family joke can cause pain
    Because it can be something that was pass down from one generation to another
        A part of a generation curse thank God He can break everything
            Chain, curse, pain and bondage
                Everything the devil tries to shame you with
                    God will make the devil pay

We as people need to learn how to slow our roll
    Stand strong and have more prayer
        God is in control of everything

What Is Your Mountain In Your Life?

The Bible says in
Matthew {17:20}

(And Jesus said unto them, Because of your unbelief: for verily I say unto you, If ye have faith as a gain of mustard seed, ye shall say unto this mountain, Remove hence to yonder place; and it shall remove; and nothing shall be impossible unto you)

Your mountain can be your supervisor, co-worker, or
A close family member, even that friend
The mountain you go through will be a mountain
you get to know

The mountain you climb can lead to more hard times; or build your faith showing you that God will carry you through

The mountain you fly over can be God blessing you to rise to a new level
Some mountains can be spiritual some can be your own pain
Some mountains can be your growth, most of all you will have a mountain,

You can have rough mountains or you can have steep ones
There may be waterfalls on your mountain
Do you recognize your mountain?

FOOT SOLDIER

Foot soldier is a person that sees potential in something or someone
When no one else can Foot loose is the one that watch and talk, because they do not understand
Foot soldier is the person that know the struggle and the pain
They will keep working to get their plans successful
Foot loose will return to see what has been done,
They make calls to talk about you to report what you have done
Foot soldier will keep praying for a person, they will stand strong in God's word
Mostly because they understand pain and hurt in the world

Don't Make A U-Turn

Matthew {7:14} Because strait is the gate, and narrow is the way, which leadeth into life and few there be that find it.

As we live our life, we may go through some bumps, bruises, even sometimes misused
No one is perfect, but we can be cautious

The path to heaven we start walking straight, then we make a U-turn
Because of fears and anxiety not realizing that God is bigger than anything we will face

A U-turn in some places, you will get a ticket
But when a Christian do a U-turn, they turn to their old ways and lose their faith
Their fear is bigger than their faith

Don't make a U-turn, turn to God, in pray and seek God's face,
So He can give you Grace

How To Love God's Child

Parents love their child or children, showing them, their love, wisdom, security and shelter
No parent enjoys seeing their children in pain or being hurt by another person

What is done in the dark will come to light.
God can see in the dark, He see the great and the small,
God will make the finally call
It is a dangerous thing to keep killing and hurting people
God will find you, surely God will have His way

We are all God's children. Just as it hurt God when people reject Jesus, it hurts when people kill one another

No one has the same exact morals
We all have God to lean on, if you want Him in your life
We should not keep rejecting God

The Earth Will Tell

The sky is dark in a shade of gray, from the sins of the men on earth
The sins that man try to hide
The moon dark reddish from the blood that was shed by men on earth
The blood of men sin that they thought that could hide
God knows all of men secret
The stars from the dimness to the brightest stars
Letting the people know that God
Is in control
Water holds the history of the past, the daker the water the greater the pain
God bless us with life to live, it is how we live, life that can cause
Destruction
There is no secret hidden from God
The earth will tell

Who Do You Report To?

People may not realize but, when you talk about someone to another person

In it is not in a positive way, then you are reporting something to another person

A dog will bring you a bone, and that same dog will carry a bone
The dog does not realize the bone was pick just for him to carry

Because the person do not want to tell you their business they will give the dog someone else information

People can live miles away, or even in another state, what someone says about you can still reach you

Lies that were told

Lies that were sow

People do not realize, God can take control of everything

Lies that were sow that is why some people is not prosper today.

Lies that were told

The devil tries to make himself look good, so he will tell anyone a lie about you

So be careful who you report to

That is why we as people need to be prayerful with everything we do and say

Take everything to God in prayer

Ditches

Basically, a ditch is a channel dug in the ground, a trench which often holds water

    A ditch can be dirty and muddy

Sad to say some people can be like that ditch, foul with nowhere to go

    Sometimes that ditch will have leaves, sticks paper and trash,

The water in the ditch will over flow

    Like someone with a trashy attitude, with a behavior out of control

A ditch can be short, long, steep or wide, it is a drainage.

    A drainage from a low line-area alongside a roadway or field

Some people forgot about their foundation no morals, value, respect and no love

    The ditch has its foundation, what about you

RAW

(Proverbs 18:12 Before destruction the heart of man is haughty, and before honor is humility)
Warning comes before destruction, to ever gang in the world today around you may go
Killing, stealing and hurting others
God knows the number of hairs on your head, He also know what's in your heart
There is not hiding place,

(Deuteronomy 29:23-24 And that the whole land thereof is brimstone, and salt, and burning, that it is not sown, nor any grass growth. Therein like the overthrow of Sodom, and Gomorrah, Admah and Zeboim which the Lord overthrow in His anger and His wrath) (24: Even all nations should say, wherefore hath the Lord done thus unto this land? What meaneth the heat of this great anger)

God don't care if you are a Democrat or Republican, He don't care about your color
We all need to show love to one another
The violence needs to stop, all over the world
Warning comes before a great destruction
Genesis [19:24] Then the Lord reign upon Sodom and Gomorrah brimstones and fire from the Lord out of heaven
Question what is in your heart, God knew everyone even before time start

Don't Let Your backbend

When you're lifting weights or picking up trash, do you let your backbend

Why is the world back bending?

I will say it again why is the world back bending

Many people in the world today seems to agree with all this sin

Man say that you cannot hit your child

God's word says in:

Proverbs {22:6} Train up a child in the way he should go: and when he gets old, he should not depart from it

The school system today has broken all of God's rules

School started because men want to teach others how to read the Bible and understand it for themselves

But sociality has allowed their back to bend now, it's all about sin

Some people in the world today, value is to control others

Standing bold in their sin

Some churches are afraid they will not tell the truth confusing people with their ways

Don't let your backbend we all need to take a stand

And stay with God's plan

www.ingramcontent.com/pod-product-compliance
Lightning Source LLC
LaVergne TN
LVHW070047070526
838200LV00028B/409